# Morecambe
# & Wise

3 5 7 9 10 8 6 4 2

First published 2003 by Ebury Press,
An imprint of Random House,
20 Vauxhall Bridge Road, London SW1V 2SA

Random House Australia (Pty) Limited
20 Alfred Street, Milsons Point, Sydney,
New South Wales 2061, Australia

Random House New Zealand Limited
18 Poland Road, Glenfield, Auckland 10, New Zealand

Random House South Africa (Pty) Limited
Endulini, 5a Jubilee Road, Parktown 2193, South Africa

The Random House Group Limited Reg. No. 954009

www.randomhouse.co.uk

Created by Essential Works
168a Camden Street, London, NW1 9PT

Printed and bound in Denmark by Nørhaven Paperback A/S, Viborg

A CIP catalogue record for this book is available from the British Library.

ISBN 0 09189455 7

Photographs: Cover, Reindeer; BBC. Cigars, Checked suits; Pictorial Press.
Bed, Skip; Thames TV. Hug; Scope

# Morecambe & Wise

their funniest jokes, one-liners and sketches

# Contents

COMEDY CLASSICS

## Who's Who?

**Morecambe, Eric**: not his real name. Took his stage name from his home town of Eric in Lancashire. Educated at Milverton Street School and held the unique honour of being the only pupil ever to obtain twelve A levels in Absenteeism. With the outbreak of World War II he served with great distinction behind the bacon counter at the Co-op, disguised as a middle-aged spinster. Worked down a coal mine where every shift he was carried in a cage to the coal face – if he turned green and fell off the perch all the other miners made a rush for the surface. Got his first break just above the ankle at the Central Pier, Birmingham, after doing the gag about the three Irishmen who wanted to start a one-man band.

**Wise, Ernie**: real name Lloyd Buttocks. Little can be said of this man that hasn't already been said by people who ought to have more respect. A man of great ingenuity, which showed itself during the Potato Famine of '35 when he invented plastic chips. Also educated at Milverton Street School where he learnt to read French and many other words besides. It was at Milverton Street School that he first showed his propensity and had to stand behind the blackboard for two hours. In 1945 he went to Hollywood and starred in many jungle films playing the part of Tarzan's left leg. Made his first stage appearance at Llandudno in *Cinderella* where he is still remembered as the finest pumpkin they ever had. Asked to name his favourite author, he smiles and with great and understandable pride shows you a signed photograph of himself.

## Introduction

**Ernie**  Good evening, ladies and
gentlemen – welcome to the book.

**Eric**  It's a sort of comical Dead Sea
Scrolls.

**Ernie**  I would like to thank you for the
money.

**Eric**  They may not be buying it, might
just be flicking through the pages
looking for the 'juicy bits'.

**Ernie**  Looking for the 'juicy bits'?

**Eric**  Like you do with the 'William' books.

**Ernie**  This isn't that sort of book, this is a
book of the highest magnitude.

**Eric**  Better than anything by Oscar and
Wilde.

**Ernie**  Exactly.

**Eric**  Better than anything by
Solzhenitsyn?

**Ernie**  Solzhenitsyn?

**Eric**  Yes.

**Ernie**  I'm not interested in ice skaters.

**Ernie**  In all modesty I think I can
safely say that this is one of the
greatest books ever written.

**Eric**  And if after reading it you are not
fully satisfied your money will be
refunded. Ern . . . Ern! Don' lie
there like that, speak to me! Ern . . .
Dearie me! Is there a doctor in the
bookshop?

## Opening Spot

**Eric**    What happens now?

**Ernie**   The opening spot from one of the
shows we did.

**Eric**    Is it any good or are you in it?

**Ernie**   They're all good. That's what this
book is all about. *The Best of
Morecambe and Wise.*

> **Eric** Should have done *The
> Worst of Morecambe and Wise.*
> Would have got twenty-
> three volumes out of it.

'This boy's a fool'

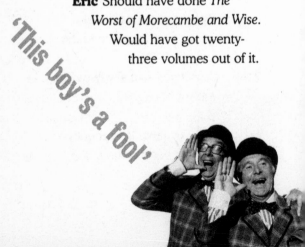

**Ernie**   I always think that the opening of any show is the most difficult, that's when you find out what the audience is going to be like.

**Eric**   I can tell right away by the look in his eye.

**Ernie**   I'm always confident.

**Eric**   I know that because you always speak the first line.

**Ernie**   Good evening, ladies and gentlemen, welcome to the show.

**Eric**   Something I've always wanted to ask you.

**Ernie**   Sorry! I never lend money to anyone because I . . .

COMEDY CLASSICS

**Eric**    No. When you say 'Good evening' etc. Do you make that up as you go along?

**Ernie**    Yes.

**Eric**    Good lord.

**Ernie**    I am a professional.

**Eric**    Saved us more than once you have. Remember that time when Nana Mouskouri came on and started singing?

**Ernie**    Never forget it.

**Eric**    Shook me – I thought he was a juggler.

> **Eric**
> *It never amazes me how so much talent can be supported on such short legs.*

## Des O'Connor Joke Number 1

**Eric** I've just bought Des O'Connor's new album.

**Ernie** Where from?

**Eric** Boots the chemist.

**Ernie** Did you need a prescription?

**Eric** I had to go to the poison counter.

### The Play What Ern Wrote

**Ernie**  Do you think I could write a
musical play?

**Eric**  You, Ern, could become another
Lionel Burke.

**Ernie**  Bart.

**Eric**  Has he? I didn't know that. Look
what *The Sound of Music* did
for Eamonn Andrews.

**Ernie**  Julie Andrews.

**Eric**  You know him better than I do.
*Showboat*. That was a great
musical. Who could ever forget
Dame Flora Robson standing on
that bale of hay and singing 'Old
Man River'? Write a musical this
afternoon about Lew Grade:
*Promises Promises*.

**Ernie**  It's been done.

**Eric**  Not by him it hasn't.

**Ernie**  Write a musical? I'm sure I could do it. Eric, are you looking at something interesting out of that window?

**Eric**  I'm just a simple fellow.

**Ernie**  That's true.

**Eric**     But to me that is the most beautiful sight that any man could ever wish to see. Ern, that is breathtaking.

**Ernie**    What is?

**Eric**     Ada Bailey hanging out her knickers on the clothes-line.

**Ernie**    Come away from that window.

*Eric opens the door. A very effeminate man enters.*

**Man**      Hello to you, old fellow.

**Eric**     Can I help you, Miss?

**Ernie**    You're the fellow who lives across the way, you called a few minutes ago.

**Man**      Yes. I thought I'd give you a ring.

*How to be like Eric:*

### The Curtain Gag 1
*You'll need floor-length curtains.
Stand behind them closed. Shout
'Are you there, Ern?' Hit the
curtains from behind and pretend
to look for the opening. After 30
seconds of fumbling, come through
the curtain with a flurry. Your hair
should be wayward and your
glasses askew.*

**Eric**   I hope you'll both be very happy
         together.

**Ernie**  My name's Ernie Wise, playwriter.
         Please sit down.

**Eric**   Take the weight off your mascara.

**Ernie**  I didn't quite get your name.

**Man**    Adrian, Adrian Fondle.

**Eric**   Sounds like a new bra.

**Man**    That's my pen name. My real name
         is Adrian Caress.

**Ernie**  Do tell about the poems what
         you're writing, Adrian.

**Man**    Well . . .

**Eric**   I do a bit of poetry writing.

**Man**    Really. How so terribly fascinating.

**Eric**    I've just finished one called 'The Fairy'. Nothing personal. My forte is monologues. I've got forty monologues in the next room.

There's a hell of a smell in Dingley Dell, The fairies are washing their socks. When up jumps a sailor . . .

**Ernie**  Why don't you shut up! Spoil everything you do! I'm so sorry about this, Mr . . .

**Man**    Call me Adrian.

**Ernie**  Call me Ern.

**Eric**    Call me tomorrow. I've had enough of this.

'This boy's a fool'.

## *Des O'Connor Sketch*

**Eric**   He's arrived.

**Ernie**   Who?

**Eric**   Do you scare easily?

**Ernie**   I watch *Crossroads*.

**Eric**   Then I can tell you that he's arrived.

**Ernie**   Who?

**Eric**   I'll give you just a little clue . . . Des O'Connor.

**Ernie**   He's in the building?

**Eric**   Yes.

**Ernie**   Are you sure?

**Eric**    When the guard dog tries to throw itself off the roof Des O'Connor must be in the building.

**Ernie**    He'll want to sing one of his songs.

**Eric**    I want to marry Raquel Welch but some things just aren't possible.

**Ernie**    God! He's coming!

**Eric**    Oh. Ladies and gentlemen, a great personal friend of ours, Des O'Connor.

**Ernie**    Des, it's a joy to see you.

**Eric**    Good old Des. Lovely to meet you at long last.

**Des**    Thank you, boys. I take it then that I am going to sing?

**Ernie**   Sing?

**Des**   Yes. I'm going to sing.

**Eric**   Well, with practice I'm sure one day
you will.

*How to be like Eric:*

### The Curtain Gag 2
*You'll need floor-length curtains.
Stand in the gap between the
closed curtains with your right side
behind the curtain. Bring your
right hand up from behind the
curtain to strangle yourself. Fight
your right hand with your left and
eventually pull yourself behind the
curtains with a tug.*

## Ernie and Money

**Eric**   That's what I like about you, you're all wallet.

**Ernie**   True. I should have been an international financier.

**Eric**   You could have been one of the gnomes of Peterborough.

**Ernie**   That's why this next sketch is one of my favourites.

**Eric**   The Bank Manager sketch.

**Ernie**   Love anything to do with banks.

**Eric**   I meant to tell you – when you go into a bank you don't have to light a candle and place it on the counter.

### The Bank Manager

**Bank Manager**   So your aunt has died
and left you this money.

**Ernie**   I'm her only living relative.

**Bank Manager**   Are you sure?

**Eric**   Positive. I just saw his leg move.

'Make the tea, Ern'

**Bank Manager** Just one moment, gentlemen. I would like to have a word with you, Mr Morecambe. In private.

**Eric** Anything you say in front of me can be said in front of him, as long as he leaves.

**Bank Manager** Please sit down. *(They sit.)* It's about your overdraft. I see that you owe the bank ten pounds.

**Eric** I've no further interest in the matter. If you look at my statement you will see that I have to my credit the sum of one thousand three hundred and seventy-three pounds.

**Bank Manager** *(Long-suffering)* Mr Morecambe, that's the date!

**Eric**   The date?

**Bank Manager**   The first of the third, seventy-three. The important figures are those here printed in red. Looking your statement, you don't seem to have regular money coming in.

**Ernie**   Well, we don't get paid regularly. We work for the BBC.

**Bank Manager**   The British Broadcasting Corporation?

**Eric**   No the Birkenhead Brick Company.

**Bank Manager**   What exactly do you do for a living?

**Ernie**   We're just entertainers.

**Eric**     We used to be on the stage before
             we closed all the variety theatres.
             We used to do jokes.

**Bank Manager**     Wisecracks?

**Eric**     I'm afraid he does these days. It's his
             age.

**Eric**     *Why don't you have a little*
             *dance?*
**Ernie**    *Actually I don't think I will*
             *– I'm a little stiff from*
             *Badminton.*
**Eric**     *It doesn't matter where*
             *you're from,  you can still*
             *join in.*

**Bank Manager**   How very curious. I write
a few jokes myself.

*Eric and Ernie have a horrified reaction.*

**Bank Manager**   Would you like to hear
one or two?

**Both**   No!

**Bank Manager**   But possibly you could
use this one in your act.

Judge in court to prisoner
– 'Have you ever been up
before me?'

Prisoner – 'I don't know,
what time do you get up
in the morning?'

*He chuckles and looks up, laughing, at the boys. There is no reaction from them and the manager's face becomes serious.*

**Bank Manager**   Could I send this to any other comedian?

**Ernie**   Send it to Jimmy Tarbuck.

**Bank Manager**   Jimmy Tarbuck? Would he use my material?

**Eric**   Why not? He uses everybody else's.

*Both exit rapidly.*

*How to be like Eric:*

**The Wig**
*With your right hand, lift the front fringe of Ernie's hair up, stare briefly and say, 'Can't see the join.'*

## Lord Ern of Peterborough

**Ernie**  (*Sits on throne.*) Lord Ern of Peterborough. That means my wife is now a Lady.

**Eric**  Give you something to do during the long winter nights.

**Ernie**  I will have to kneel before the Queen.

**Eric**  She'll never reach you with a sword.

**Ernie**  I'll have to move to a big posh house. Tea on the lawn, eating croquet.

**Eric**  You'll like them. Especially the well-done ones.

**Ernie**  Cowes over the weekend.

**Eric**   You dirty little devil. Of course, you'll need a monogram.

**Ernie**   I'll have no time for playing records.

**Eric**   That's true.

**Ernie**   I'll buy my mother a new home.

**Eric**   Nothing wrong with the one you bought her last year. Plenty of room if the dog rolls over.

**Ernie**   I can't live in the flat now.

**Eric**   Now you're being selfish. Who's the cat going to play with if you go?

**Ernie**   I suppose my wife will want a daily.

**Eric**   You'll have to get a sailor in, then.

> ### How to Treat a Celebrity the Morecambe & Wise Way:
>
> **Pretend that they are their greatest rivals, for instance insist that Peter Cushing is Christopher Lee and vice versa.**

## Des O'Connor Joke Number 2

**Eric**    Have you got any plans for the future?

**Ernie**    I'd like to do something with Des O'Connor.

**Eric**    So would I but how can we lure him to the riverbank without him suspecting?

## High Finance

Ernie   Shut up and leave me to work in peace. I'm engrossed in high finance.

**Eric**   High finance.

Ernie   Yes.

**Eric**   With those legs? Impossible. I've been with you when you've gone into the bank, your little head just sticking up over the top of the counter and all the bank clerks whispering to one another – 'Sooty's back.'

## How to Treat a Celebrity the Morecambe & Wise Way:

Make them think that they're getting a solo spot on the show. And then steal the number. I.e. when Shirley Bassey (always call her Burly Chassis, by the way) loses a shoe during a number, crawl behind a part of the scenery, shuffle up behind her, take off your boot and put it on her.

### Famous Guests – Vanessa Redgrave

**Ernie**  My famous play about Napoleon next.

**Eric**  With Vanessa Redcoat?

**Ernie**  Redgrave. She gave us a few problems.

**Eric**  With her being such a tall girl?

**Ernie**  Do you know she wanted paying by the inch?

**Eric**  We'd have been skint. A delightful lady to work with.

**Ernie**  Affable.

**Eric**   Always thought she was British.

**Ernie**   She worked hard at rehearsal.

**Eric**   Did you see her during the breaks?
She was stretched out fast asleep in
three separate dressing rooms.

**Ernie**   Vanessa rather liked me.

**Eric**   Oh?

> **Eric**   *That girl's got
> two of the ugliest
> legs in town.*
> **Ernie**   *How do you
> know?*
> **Eric**   *I've counted
> them.*

**Ernie**  Offered me a lift home in her car.

**Eric**  Fool!

**Ernie**  What do you mean?

**Eric**  It was only because she didn't have a dipstick.

**Ernie**  This is a play of mine we did in one of our Christmas shows with Vanessa Redgrave.

**Eric**  We wanted a big bird for Christmas and we got one.

'What do you think of it so far?' 'Ruggish'

## Napoleon & Josephine with Vanessa Redgrave

*Scene: in the richly furnished tent used by Napoleon on the battlefield of Waterloo. Tent is deserted. F/X heavy gunfire and the distant shouting of men in battle. Ernie enters as Napoleon: staggers around the tent before standing still and looking very distressed.*

**Ernie** Sacré Beaujolais! That it should come to this – that I, Napoleon Bonaparte, the tenacious Corsican, should come to this. Defeated by that devil, Wellington. Sacré Beaujolais and bon appetite.

*Ernie bows his head and is sobbing . . . as Vanessa Redgrave enters as Josephine, looking seductive. She stops and sees Ernie sobbing.*

**Vanessa** He is crying again. I wish he wouldn't cry. The tears roll down his legs and make them shrink. I do love him. When he kisses me I can feel his heart beating against my kneecaps.

*She crosses to Ernie and places an arm on his shoulder.*

**Vanessa** Napoleon, sit down.

**Ernie** I am sat down.

**Vanessa** Napoleon, my beloved, tell your Josephine what has happened.

**Ernie** The flower of the French Army lies crushed upon the battlefield of Waterloo. I have lost some of my finest men.

**Vanessa** What about the big red-headed
drummer lad?

**Ernie** What?

**Vanessa** The one with the big cymbals.

**Ernie** Oh him. Gone. Your Napoleon has
been defeated.

**Vanessa** You must have known in your
heart that defeat was inevitable.

**Ernie** I must be honest, two nights ago I
had a slight inkling.

**Vanessa** Why didn't you tell me? I was
awake. I take it that you have lost
to the Duke of Wellington.

**Ernie** He is at this very moment on his
way here with the terms of the
surrender.

*Sounds of horses' hoofs. Eric enters as
Wellington. Hoofs continue.*

**Eric**   That horse never stops . . . Evenin'
all. Sorry I'm late. Some fool kept
me talking. Said he wanted to
name a rubber boot after me. The
Duke of Wellington at your service.

*Eric salutes. Ernie salutes; pulls rabbit out of
jacket.*

**Ernie**   Napoleon Bonaparte.

**Eric**   *(Walks past Vanessa to Ernie.)* I
don't want to worry you but this
tent pole's loose.

**Ernie**   How dare you, sir? That tent pole
is the Empress Josephine.

*Ernie places a small box in front of Vanessa.
He stands on it and faces her.*

**Ernie**   Tell him who you are.

**Vanessa**   I am indeed the Empress
Josephine of France.

**Ernie**   And what are you doing up at the
front? Not that it matters – it suits
you.

**Vanessa**   The Emperor wishes to discuss the
Battle of Waterloo.

**Eric**   Odd name for a battle. There was
no water and I couldn't find a . . .

**Ernie**   *(Getting off box.)* How dare you!

**Vanessa**   Boney, my darling.

**Ernie**   Not tonight, Josephine.

**Eric**   What does he mean?

> ### How to Treat a Celebrity the Morecambe & Wise Way:
>
> **Make them feel grateful to be on the show. Tell them that you are their greatest fan (and then get their identity wrong). Tell them about the other great stars who've appeared. I.e. telling Peter Barkworth that 'We had that nice Sir John Mills on, you know.'**

**Ernie**   It is of little consequence.

**Vanessa**   *(Looking at Eric.)* I'll second that.

**Vanessa**   We are alone.

**Eric**   Ready when you are, pally.

**Vanessa** Poor Napoleon, he's been going through a bad time. Since his retreat from Moscow, he's been very cold towards me.

**Eric** Well, with that deep snow and those short legs . . . say no more. *(Nudges Vanessa.)* Would um . . . *(Moves centre, to bed.)* . . . would you like something to warm you up?

**Vanessa** I would very much.

**Eric** Good. I think I've got some extra-strong mints in my greatcoat.

**Vanessa** I think no. Wellie . . .?

**Eric** Yes.

**Vanessa** Napoleon has been so engrossed in the battle that he's tended to neglect me.

**Eric**    Oh.

**Vanessa** I am a woman.

**Eric**    Have you told him?

**Vanessa** I like you. *(She sprays perfume on to her neck.)* 'Midnight in Paris'.

**Eric**    *(Picks up bottle and dabs his cheeks with it.)* Two fifteen in Darlington – just before the kick-off.

'Look at me when I'm talking to you. Oh, you are'

## *Summer Night in the Garden*

**Eric**    Lovely day for it, Ern.

**Ernie**    Lovely day for it?

**Eric**    If you like.

**Ernie**    No jokes. *(Pause.)* It's hot.

**Eric**    It's the heat.

**Ernie**    Take a chair.

**Eric**    I've got one at home.

**Ernie**    Just sit down.

**Eric**    I'd rather stand. *(He sits down.)*
Garden looks nice.

**Ernie**    Good.

**Eric**   I like those red flowers, the geronimos.

**Ernie**   Geraniums. *(Pause.)* It's hot.

**Eric**   It's the heat. Nice music.

**Ernie**   Delius.

**Eric**   Is he British?

**Ernie**   Bradford.

**Eric**   Could have sworn he was British. *(Pause, then looks up pointing.)* Woodpecker.

**Ernie**   Woodpecker?

**Eric**   Just flown out of that tree.

**Ernie**   How do you know it was a woodpecker?

**Eric**    I could smell the cider. *(Chuckles.)*

**Ernie**   Please.

*Pause.*

**Eric**    What do they call those little tiny
            insects with lots of legs?

**Ernie**   Don't know and I don't care.

**Eric**    You should.

**Ernie**   Why?

**Eric**    One of them's just crawled up the
            leg of your shorts.

**Ernie**   *(Leaps to his feet.)* What!

**Eric**    *(Laughing.)* That's what's known as
            a journey into the unknown.

*How to be like Eric:*

### The Slap

*Put your left hand on Ernie's right shoulder and your right hand on his left shoulder. Tilt your head slightly to the right. With open palms, slap Ernie's cheeks. Twice if you think you can get away with it. Turn right, stare at the camera and say, 'This boy's a fool!'*

## Escape from Stalag 54 with John Mills

**Eric**  Before I go – if I don't come back will you please give this parcel to my wife?

**John Mills**  But you will come back.

**Eric**  In case I don't, please see that my wife gets this parcel.

**Ernie**  But what is it?

**Eric**  A hand grenade.

## *Bed Sketch*

*Ernie is in bed, wearing his pyjamas and writing in a notebook. Eric is on top of the bed, with his dressing gown over pyjamas. He is reading* Yoga for Better Health.

**Ernie** *(Stops writing and looks puzzled.)* How do you spell incompetent?

**Eric** E-R-N-I-E.

**Ernie** E-R . . . *(Realising)* Oh!

**Eric** Taking shape is it?

**Ernie** Just got to the part where Inspector Darling of New Scotland Yard has just . . .

**Eric** Who?

> ### *How to Treat a Celebrity the Morecambe & Wise Way:*
>
> *Tell them how to do their job. Tell actors to speak out properly and not be afraid. Tell singers that you'll be there, don't worry.*

**Ernie**  I'm creating a new character, Guy Darling, ace detective. It starts off where he's been followed by two men.

**Eric**  I'm not surprised.

**Ernie**  I've just got to the part where he's arrived at The Grange to arrest the fellow what did it.

**Eric**  To arrest the man what did it?

**Ernie**  My first thriller.

**Eric**  That's long overdue. *(Reads for a few seconds then looks up.)* Agatha Crusty.

**Ernie**  Who?

**Eric**  Agatha Crusty. He wrote thrillers.

**Ernie**  Did he?

**Eric**  Oh yes. He wrote that one that's been running in London now for about ninety years . . . *The Black and White Minstrels.*

**Ernie**  George Mitchell.

**Eric**  I never knew he wrote thrillers!

*Ernie looks puzzled, then continues to write. He stops and looks up.*

**Ernie**  What's yours like?

**Eric**  Pardon?

**Ernie**  The book.

**Eric**  Yoga.

**Ernie**  That's not for me.

**Eric**  You know a lot about yoga then?

**Ernie**  Only that it's made from milk.

*Ernie continues to write . . . Eric looks puzzled.*

**Eric**   *(After a pause.)* Indians.

**Ernie**   What about them?

**Eric**   They're good at yoga.

**Ernie**   Oh.

**Eric**   It's way of life out there. It's their bingo.

**Ernie**   Oh, that sort of yoga. I once read that proper yoga fellows in India can sit cross-legged on the floor for twenty-four hours without moving a muscle.

**Eric**    After four bowls of curry you'd be
            frightened to move a muscle. Has
            he arrived at The Grange yet?

**Ernie**   Inspector Darling of New Scotland
            Yard?

**Eric**    Yes.

**Ernie**   *(Taps notebook.)* Just finished that
            bit. Listen to this . . . *(Reads from
            notebook.)* Inspector Darling rang
            the front doorbell. After a pause of
            some few seconds Lady Angela
            opened the door with a smile.

**Eric**    That's a good trick.

**Ernie**   *(Still reading.)* He entered the study
            to find Sir Digby, skewered to the
            floor with a twelve-inch dagger.

**Eric**    Powerful stuff. You could be another

– what's his name? – you know, they
called him 'the bard'.

Ernie  The one who wrote all those
       sonnets and odes?

Eric   No, not Cyril Fletcher. There's an
       exercise here and it says after it in
       big red letters underlined 'When in
       this position do not yodel.' The last
       time I saw a position like that was at
       the Odeon.

Ernie  *(Closes notebook.)* I'm tired.

Eric   And no wonder, the way you drive
       yourself. Words cascade from your
       pen like pearls from a broken
       necklace.

Ernie  I'm dead beat.

Eric   Have you cleaned your tooth?

**Ernie**   I'm going to settle down.

**Eric**   Get married?

**Ernie**   Sleep.

**Eric**   What about Inspector Darling?

**Ernie**   He's just put a tail on the gardener.

**Eric**   That'll keep the flies off his dahlias.
*(Laughs.)*

**Ernie**   *(Settles down.)* Good night, Eric.

**Eric**   *(Looking at yoga book.)* By golly
some of these positions are
impossible – fine if you're a jelly
baby. *(Turns book to get a better
view of an illustration.)* I wouldn't
fancy doing that on cold lino.
Impossible. *(Closes book and places
it on the bedside table.)* Goodnight.

## Famous Guests – Cliff Richard

*Eric gets a banana, with string tied round it for a cable: Eric 'tests' the banana for sound, and gives it to Cliff. Cliff sings 'Livin' Doll' while Eric and Ernie start dancing. Cliff stops singing and watches the boys, looking rather worried.*

**Cliff**    Boys, I don't know how to say this.

**Eric**    Don't say anything.

**Ernie**    We know it's good.

**Cliff**    Yes, it's . . . but don't you think . . . what you're doing is a little old-fashioned.

*Long horrified pause.*

**Cliff**    What I mean is . . . I'm singing a sort of new type of song and your routine is very old.

*Another long pause.*

**Cliff**   I mean . . . in any case, I saw you do
           the same thing with Tom Jones.

**Both**   Who?

**Cliff**   Tom Jones.

**Ernie**   Oh, that six-footer, curly hair, well
           set up.

**Eric**   Thought that was Nina.

**Cliff**   Can we do one of Ernie's plays?

**Ernie**   No.

*Moves right with disgust.*

**Eric**   You've offended him now.

## How to Treat a Celebrity the Morecambe & Wise Way:

*Serious Actors – Always refer to them as Sir or Dame if they are neither, and always refer to actual Knights of the Realm and Dames (such as Sir Ralph Richardson or Flora Robson) as Your Highness and make a small curtsy when shaking hands.*

**Cliff**    I was thinking of something a bit more 'with it' – like this.

*Cliff dances.*

**Eric**    We don't want to get laughs!

**Ernie**    Three American sailors on board a battleship doing a dance routine with mops.

**Eric**    Never been done before.

**Cliff**    Never been done before! But didn't I see Gene Kelly do that in a film?

**Ernie**    Never.

**Eric**    Gene Kelly. She'd never dress up as an American sailor.

**Ernie**    Not now that she's Princess Grace of Meccano.

**Cliff**   I didn't realise.

**Eric**   Be guided by us.

**Cliff**   Well all right then, we'll do it your way. But are you sure it's going to work?

*Eric takes the banana from him and eats it.*

**Eric**   If you're really worried we'll get that singing group at the back of you – Olivier, Newton and John. Three nice fellows.

### Famous Guests – Dame Flora Robson

*Eric is a butler, Ernie the Lord of the Manor House that they have borrowed in order to impress their guest, Dame Flora Robson.*

*Dame Flora enters. She holds a parasol on her shoulder. Eric closes sliding door behind her as she walks forward – the parasol is cut in half and she is left holding just a stick.*

**Ernie**  Dame Flora. I'm delighted to meet you.

**Dame Flora**  Are you Mr Wise?

**Ernie**  Most of the time *(Takes her hand.)*

**Eric**  Could I have your coat, please?

**Ernie**  You got my message then, Dame Flora.

**Dame Flora**     Yes I did. When I arrived
                   here at the airport, inviting
                   me to have drinks with you
                   in this house.

**Eric**     Could I have your coat please,
             sweetheart?

Ernie     It is a rather beautiful house, isn't it?

**Dame Flora**     I'm rather surprised to see
                   you in such beautiful
                   surroundings.

Ernie     Well, you see, Dame Flora, when one
          is a successful writer like what I am,
          one can afford a residence like this.

**Eric**     Are you going to give me that coat
             or not?

Ernie     You like my little place then, Dame
          Flora?

**Dame Flora**    I do. I like it very much indeed, Mr Wise. When I received your note I . . . *(Stops because Eric is pulling at the sleeve of her coat, trying to remove it.)*

**Ernie**  Eric, please!

**Dame Flora**    Oh, I'm so sorry. I didn't realise you were waiting to take my coat.

*Eric helps her remove her coat.*

**Eric**  The heating is full on you know.

**Ernie**  This is Eric, my butler. The old family retriever.

**Dame Flora**    *(Mystified)* Family retriever?

**Eric** *Doctor, could you give me some sleeping pills for my wife?*

**Ernie** *Why?*

**Eric** *She keeps waking up.*

**Eric**   It's the ears that do it. If you whistle for me five miles away, I'll come running.

**Ernie**   That's right. *(Turns back on Eric as he indicates that Dame Flora be seated on the settee.)* Dame Flora, please be sat down.

*Eric puts her coat over Ernie's shoulders.*

**Dame Flora**   *(Sits.)* Thank you.

**Ernie**   As you may know Dame Flora, I have written an absolutely brilliant play.

*Ernie sits on the sofa next to Dame Flora.*

**Dame Flora**   You've got my coat on, Mr Wise.

**Ernie**   No, that's not the title. *(Realises.)*

Oh, I'm most terribly, awfully sorry.
*(Ernie rises, Eric helps him off with
the coat. Eric folds coat and puts it
on settee, Ernie sits on it.)* You have
a coat like this, don't you, Dame
Flora? So sorry Dame Flora,
everything's slightly adjacent today.

**Dame Flora**    *(Mystified)* Slightly adjacent?

**Ernie**  I'm glad you've noticed.

**Dame Flora**    Tell me about your play, Mr
Wise.

**Ernie**  It's historical and it also takes place
in the past. We're so pleased that
you're considering appearing in my
play, and we're even more delighted
that you've agreed to do it for
nothing.

**Dame Flora**    I'm doing it for nothing?

**Ernie**  That's very kind of you.

**Eric**  That was a clever one, Ern. Can I have the keys to the wine closet, please?

**Ernie**  They're in my pocket. Excuse me Dame, Dame Flora.

*Gives Eric the end of a key chain. Through the next speech Eric moves over to the drinks cabinet and we see a very long piece of string being pulled out of Ernie's pocket.*

**Ernie**   I've always been an ardent admirer
of your work, the chance to work
with you has always been my
greatest ambition. *(Ernie is pulled
completely off the settee.)* I'm
terribly sorry, I slipped off the settee.

**Dame Flora**   Have you hurt yourself?

**Ernie**   No, only when I laugh.

**Eric**   *(Giving bottle and glasses to Dame
Flora.)* Would you mind holding
these?

*Eric sets the table and drinks during the next
speech.*

**Ernie**   About my play, Dame Flora. It deals
with Her Most Gracious Majesty
Queen Elizabeth I.

**Dame Flora**   That sounds very interesting. I've always thought that the reign of Queen Elizabeth I covered one of the most colourful periods in our history.

**Eric**   Would you care for a drink, sir?

**Ernie**   Ladies first.

**Eric**   I know. Would you care for a drink, sir?

**Ernie**   Thank you.

**Eric**   Say when. *(Starts pouring.)*

**Ernie**   *(Ignoring Eric)* I quite agree with you that this is a most interesting part of our history and in the way I've written this play I have tried to bring out the characters of not only

Queen Elizabeth but the people
surrounding her at court.

**Eric**   (*Interrupting*) There's a man coming
to give you some money.

**Ernie**   When?

**Eric**   (*Stops pouring.*) Never fails. (*Turns to
Dame Flora.*) Would you like a quick
snort my lord?

**Ernie**   (*Aside*) Oh God.

**Dame Flora**   I beg your pardon?

**Eric**   Would you care for a drop of falling-
down water?

**Dame Flora**   Yes, a little please. (*Eric
pours.*) Thank you, that's
plenty.

**Eric**    It's all you're going to get. I can recommend it – it's the eighty-three.

**Dame Flora**    Eighty-three?

**Eric**    Eighty-three bottles for fifteen and nine.

**Ernie**    Here's to a happy association. *(They clink glasses and drink.)*

**Eric**    Would you like a little more?

**Ernie**    Just a little touch.

**Eric**    Later. But are you going to have some more drink?

**Ernie**    Yes please. *(Eric pours.)*

**Eric** *Who's your tailor?*

**Ernie** *Why?*

**Eric** *That was my second question.*

'Make the tea, Ern'

**Eric** *(To Dame Flora)* How about you your reverence?

**Dame Flora** *(Placing hand over top of glass.)* No, I don't think so.

*Eric pours drink and it goes over Dame Flora's hand.*

**Eric** I do beg your pardon, my lord. *(Shakes Dame Flora's hand over bottle.)*

**Ernie** You stupid idiot.

**Eric** I shouldn't stand for that. Did it go over your dress?

**Dame Flora** No, it didn't touch my dress. It went over my hand and melted the strap of my wristwatch.

**Eric**  *(To Ern)* We've got a right one here.
I told you it was good. One glass of
that stuff and you'll break the sound
barrier.

*How to be like Eric:*

**The Doorbell
(or Telephone)**
*Whenever the doorbell (or
telephone) rings, stare
amazed at Ernie and say,
'How do you do that?'*

### *Eric & Ern on Dame Flora*

**Ernie**  After that performance by Dame Flora I've got to admit you were right.

**Eric**  'Course I was. I told you when you first started to write that play about Queen Elizabeth that Dame Flora was a better bet than Larry Grayson.

**Ernie**  I suppose he does go over the top.

**Eric**  Just a bit. When you write your life story don't forget to say that you had one of the all-time greats in one of your plays.

**Ernie**  I will.

**Eric**  And make sure you spell my name right.

**Ernie** Dame Flora Robson is a perfectionist – the magnificent costume she wore in that play.

**Eric** Proper regal robes of the period they were.

**Ernie** Anyone could see that.

**Eric** Six hours she was in the launderette with that lot.

**Ernie** Dame Flora looked absolutely magnificent, beautiful frock that was.

**Eric** More sequins on that frock than you'll see in sixteen programmes of *Come Dancing*.

**Ernie** We've been very lucky, Eric. The great stars we've had working with us. Dame Flora and next the great Glenda Jackson as Cleopatra.

**Eric**    A fine lady actor.

**Ernie**    You see if I'm not right, one of these days they'll make Glenda a Dame.

**Eric**    No, she won't do pantomime now. She's internationally famous now, she's got half as many awards as you.

**Ernie**    Didn't know she was that good.

**Eric**    She's got two Oscars.

**Ernie**    Didn't even know she was married. I do know she did a very good job as Cleopatra in my play of the same name.

**Eric**    What was the play called?

**Ernie**    I think it was *Cleopatra*.

**Eric**    Oh.

**Ernie**    She gave my work a certain tone, a certain dignity.

**Eric**    So that's what ruined it.

'This boy's a fool'

## Famous Guests – Cleopatra with Glenda Jackson

*Eric enters to signature music of* Match of the Day. *He is dressed as a gladiator and wearing wellington boots and a busby. Fade music.*

**Eric**  Evenin' all! Sorry I'm late only I've been irrigating the desert – takes a bit of doing on your own.

**Glenda**  Is Caesar with you?

**Eric**  No he couldn't come. He's got the hieroglyphics.

**Glenda**  You must be hungry after such a long journey – can I get you some food?

**Eric**  Thank you all the same but I've just had a couple of sheep's eyes – they'll see me through the day.

**Glenda**  (*Seductively*) But you must be
hungry for something.

**Eric**  That's true.

**Ernie**  And what is your business here?

**Eric**  I have been sent from Julius and
Caesar.

**Glenda**  Julius and Caesar?

**Eric**  I'm afraid so – a slight accident
whilst polishing his sword.

**Glenda**  Am I right in assuming that you
have been sent here with the sole
object of spying on me?

**Eric**  Is there anything to spy on?

**Glenda**  Meaning?

**Eric**     You and the little chap here, have
             you been . . . touch of the hello
             folks?

**Ernie**    Good heavens no, sir! How could
             you think such a thing! Nothing of
             that nature going on here I do
             assure you most sincerely.

**Glenda**   All men are fools, and what makes
             them so is having beauty like what
             I have got.

**Eric**     You have a plan?

**Glenda**   Let me have five minutes alone
             with him. If I can incriminate him
             we need have no fear of what he
             can do.

**Ernie**    He is a dedicated Roman soldier
             and you will never implicate him.

**Ernie** Can you telephone from an aeroplane?

**Eric** Everyone can tell a phone from an aeroplane, can't they?

**Glenda**   Leave me alone with him.

**Ernie**   *(To Eric)* Would you like me to attend to your camel?

**Eric**   It's outside – can't miss it – looks like a horse with an airlock. *(Gives Ernie the hat.)* Put this on his hump in case it freezes during the night.

**Ernie**   Right away! *(Exits.)*

**Eric**   A remarkable beast.

**Glenda**   The camel?

**Eric**   No, Ern.

*Oboe plays oriental music as Glenda moves seductively to the bed.*

> **How to Treat a Celebrity the Morecambe & Wise Way:**
> *Always get their name confused. For instance, call André Previn, André Preview.*

**Eric**    Is your back still bad?

**Glenda**    I like you.

**Eric**    Hello.

## *Famous Guests – André Preview (a letter from the conductor)*

My relationship with Eric and Ernie is not the usual conductor-to-soloist relationship. While it is true that Eric did play the Grieg Piano Concerto for me, and while it is true that, during a return engagement, both the gentlemen sang while I conducted, it must be said that our pattern of work habits differs from the norm.

When we have the ordinary, run-of-the-mill soloist with the London Symphony Orchestra, we waste a lot of time at rehearsals talking about mundane, boring things such as the varying interpretive fine points of the repertoire, the musicological background of the work involved, opinions on phrasing and tempos, all that kind of unnecessary nonsense. On the other hand, I remember distinctly that during my first rehearsal with Eric and Ernie I spent quite a lot of the time defending myself, because I would not start the orchestra by going 'a-one, a-two'!! The rest of the rehearsal time was taken up by a discussion on the varying fine points of several ventriloquists we had all seen recently.

The boys have always been extremely kind and courteous to me. I want to give you an example of that: Eric never fails to apologise both before and after he hits me. I have been given to understand that they will ask me to work with them again, as soon as they can think of further humiliations to put me through. What's more, I look forward to it a great deal.

*André Previn*

### *Famous Guests – Eric & Ern on André Previn*

**Ernie**  As a matter of fact we did have him on one of our shows. Andy Preview.

**Eric**  Charming man but a rotten pianist.

**Ernie**  Andy Preview a rotten pianist!!

**Eric**  So you heard!
Keep it to yourself. He has got a living to make. He never went near the black notes.

> **Eric** *I broke my leg in three places.*
>
> **Ernie** *Didn't anyone warn you about going to those places?*

**Ernie**  Not once. He kept asking for an arpeggio.

**Eric**  He did and we said we'd eat later. Between us, Gladys Mills would leave him standing and you'd get more to the pound.

## It's a Dog's Life!

**Eric**  I could never get rid of a dog. I'll never forget having our last one put down.

**Ernie**  Was he mad?

**Eric**  He was furious! And we'd been such pals. Every day we used to go for a tramp in the woods.

**Ernie**  I bet he enjoyed that!

**Eric**  He did. Mind you, the tramp was getting a bit fed up. He was such a clever dog, too. The only dog I ever had that could say its own name.

**Ernie**  What was it called?

**Eric**   Woof. You remember the film *Lassie Come Home*?

**Ernie**   Yes.

**Eric**   He was in that.

**Ernie**   What part did he play?

**Eric**   The lead. I was in it too, actually – I had a bit part.

**Ernie**   What did you do?

**Eric**   I got bit. This dog ran up to me, barking its head off . . .

**Ernie**   But didn't you know, a barking dog never bites?

**Eric**   I did – but the dog didn't.

### This Is a Mix-up!

**Eric**   Excuse me, can you see a policeman round here?

**Ernie**   No.

**Eric**   Okay, stick 'em down!

**Ernie**   You mean stick 'em up!

**Eric**   Don't confuse me – I'm nervous enough as it is. Just give me your watch.

**Ernie**   But it isn't worth anything. Its only value is sentimental.

**Eric**   Let's have it anyway – I feel like a good cry. I'll never forget my mother's words to me when I first went to jail.

**Ernie**   What did she say?

**Eric**   Hello, son.

**Ernie**   What were you in for?

**Eric**   Well, I'd started in a small way –
picking midgets' pockets.

**Ernie**   How could you stoop so low?

**Eric**   Stoop? I was up on tiptoe! I was
very young. I can remember it to
this day, being hustled into the back
door of the court with my nappy
over my head to avoid the
photographers.

## Bottom of the Pops!

**Ernie**  Would you like to read my new novel? I've got a copy here, hot off the press.

**Eric**  I'd love to – I very much enjoyed your last book. Who wrote it for you?

**Ernie**  I'm so glad you liked it. Who read it to you?

**Eric**  No, but seriously, I've nothing but admiration for you as a writer. And I've very little of that.

**Ernie**  What you don't seem to realise is that I am, deep down, a very intelligent person. In fact I was just about the most intelligentest person in my school.

**Eric**　So you actually did go to school?

**Ernie**　Of course I did. When it came to education my father wanted me to have all the opportunities he never had.

**Eric**　So what did he do?

**Ernie**　He sent me to a girls' school.

**Eric**　I bet you gave your teacher a lot of trouble.

**Ernie**　I did. I was always giving her trouble. Once she had to send for my father to make me behave. Then she had to send for my mother to make my father behave.

**Eric**　He sounds like quite a lad, your father.

**Ernie** Oh, he is. He knows how to make a peach cordial.

**Eric** How?

**Ernie** He buys her a drink. But he wasn't always like that. Before he got married they used to call him 'jigsaw'.

**Eric** Why 'jigsaw'?

**Ernie** 'Cos every time he was faced with a young lady he used to go to pieces. If my dad hadn't been so shy and reserved I'd be at least four years older.

**Eric** So how did he meet your mother?

**Ernie** They were first cousins.

**Eric** First cousins?

**Ernie** You were driving
down a one-way
street.

**Eric** But I was only
driving one way.

'This boy's a fool'

**Ernie** Yes, that's why I look so much alike.

**Eric** I understand they're in the iron and steel business?

**Ernie** That's right – she irons and he steals. But at the time that they got married, he was a jerry-builder and she was a chambermaid. It was a sort of marriage of convenience.

**Eric** How did your father like children?

**Ernie** Boiled. One day a bloke came to the door and he said, 'I'm collecting for Doctor Barnardo's.'

**Eric** So did your father give him anything?

**Ernie** Yes, five of us.

**Eric** Maybe you weren't doing enough to please him.

**Ernie**  I did try. I remember one cold, wet night when he was coming in late from work, I lit a big roaring fire in his bedroom.

**Eric**  Was he pleased?

**Ernie**  Of course he wasn't.

**Eric**  Why not?

**Ernie**  There wasn't a fireplace in his bedroom. Finally, I could stand it no longer, so I ran away from home.

**Eric**  You ran away?

**Ernie**  Yes, and it took them six months to find me.

**Eric**  Six months? Why?

**Ernie**  They didn't look.

**Eric**    But wasn't your father upset at the thought of you leaving home?

**Ernie**    Poor Dad, I remember his last words.

**Eric**    What were they?

**Ernie**    'Rover,' he said.

**Eric**    'Rover'?

**Ernie**    Yes, he'd always wanted a dog. 'Rover,' he said, 'when are you leaving?' And I said, 'I'm leaving tomorrow, Dad.'

**Eric**    And what did he say?

**Ernie**    He said, 'Son, don't leave us tomorrow, please.'

**Eric**    How sad.

# 'What do you think of it so far?' 'Ruggish'

**Ernie**  'Leave us today.'

**Eric**  I wonder what made him like that.

**Ernie**  I think it all stems from his disappointment when I was born.

**Eric**  Why? Did he want a girl?

**Ernie**  No, he wanted a divorce. And from then on he always seemed to be disappointed in me. I remember once he said to me, 'How old are you, son?' And I said, 'I'm five.'

**Eric**  And what was his reply?

**Ernie**  He was furious. He said, 'You ought to be ashamed of yourself. Why, when I was your age I was ten.' I realised I'd have to do better in the future.

**Eric**  So what did you do?

**Ernie**  I said to him, 'Dad, can I have an encyclopedia?'

**Eric**  Did you get one?

**Ernie**  No. He said, 'Of course you can't – you can walk to school like all the other kids.'

**Eric**  You must have really hated him.

**Ernie**  I did. And what made me hate him even more than anything else was the way he made me get up every morning at six to feed the chickens.

**Eric**  Why did you hate him so much for that?

**Ernie**  Why did I hate him so much for it? We didn't have any chickens.

'Make the tea, Ern'

## *Tee for Two!*

**Ernie**  But seriously, what do you think of
my game?

**Eric**  It's terrific. Mind you, I still prefer
golf. You know what your main
trouble is?

**Ernie**  What?

**Eric**  You stand too close to the ball after
you've hit it.

## Life with the Lions!

**Ernie**  Did you have to go deep into the
jungle?

**Eric**  Certainly, we went to places where
the hand of man has never set foot.
Deep, deep in the jungle, where the
young girls all wear grass skirts and
the young men spend all their time
saving up for lawnmowers.

**Ernie**  Did you meet any wild animals?

**Eric**  Yes – one day we came face to face
with a ferocious lion.

**Ernie**  Did it give you a start?

**Eric**  I didn't need one. But I'd read a
book about lions so I knew exactly
which steps to take.

**Ernie**    What?

**Eric**    Long ones. I ran to the nearest tree
and climbed up it.

**Ernie**    What about your wife?

**Eric**    She wasn't so lucky. The lion seized
her in his jaws and carried her off.

**Ernie**    Good heavens! What did she do?

**Eric**    She cried out, 'Shoot! Shoot!'

**Ernie**    And did you?

**Eric**    I couldn't.

**Ernie**    Why?

**Eric**  I'd run out of film.

**Ernie**  Did you get down from the tree?

**Eric**  No, you get down from a swan –
you get wood from a tree.

**Ernie**  Weren't you a
twin?
**Eric**  I was – our
parents couldn't
afford to have us
one at a time.

## Fighting Mad

**Ernie**   What are those medals you're wearing?

**Eric**   These are my military medals – I won them during the war.

**Ernie**   I didn't know you'd won a couple of medals – what were they for?

**Eric**   Well, this one I got for saving two women.

**Ernie**   Saving two women?

**Eric**   Yes, one for myself and one for the general.

**Ernie**   And what about the other one?

**Eric**   Ah, yes, this was for saving the lives of the entire regiment.

**Ernie**  What did you do?

**Eric**  I shot the cook.

**Ernie**  I don't believe you were wounded at all. Have you any scars?

**Eric**  No, but I can lend you a cigarette.

**Ernie**  But did you actually see any action?

**Eric**  You're talking to a man who spent 1944 as driver and stage manager for Big Betty Braithwaite's All-Girl Yodelling Belly Dancers and you're asking me if I saw any action. Please!

## *Tight Christmas*

**Ernie**  Well, the festive season is here again. Are you doing anything special?

**Eric**  Not really. We're having my mother-in-law for lunch on Christmas Day.

**Ernie**  How nice.

**Eric**  Yes, I prefer chicken myself but times are hard. And I'm getting the wife a surprise present.

**Ernie**  What is it?

**Eric**  A packet of cigarettes.

**Ernie**  That's not much of a surprise.

**Eric**  It is – she's expecting a fur coat.

**Ernie**   And what am I getting from you this
Christmas?

**Eric**   Close your eyes and what do you
see?

**Ernie**   Nothing.

'Look at me when I'm talking to you. Oh, you are'

**Eric**   Well, that's what you're getting.

**Ernie**   Was it a big family?

**Eric**   I'll say. I was the fourteenth out of thirteen children. And born in a pretty tough area too. If you saw a cat with a tail on round our way, you knew he was a tourist. Even the doctor who delivered me was poor – his stethoscope was on a party line. I remember one year my parents couldn't afford to buy me the pair of shoes they'd promised me.

**Ernie**   So what did they do?

**Eric**   They painted my feet black and laced up my toes.

## How to Treat a Celebrity the Morecambe & Wise Way:

**Tell them that they could have gotten a rival on the show for less money, i.e. telling Cilla Black that 'We could have had Lulu for a quid less, you know.'**

## School Daze!

**Ernie**   I didn't know you had a brother.

**Eric**   Of course you did. I've told you before, my parents had three children. One of each.

**Ernie**   What are their names?

**Eric**   Well, there's my brother – he's named after my father.

**Ernie**   What do you call him?

**Eric**   Dad. And there's my sister, Onyx.

**Ernie**   Onyx. Why did they call her Onyx?

**Eric**   'Cos she was Onyxpected. She was one of the prettiest babies in our town.

**Ernie**  Really? Where did she first see the light of day?

**Eric**  Well, she first saw the light of day in Stockport. She was actually born two years earlier in Manchester.

'Make the tea, Ern'

## Girl Talk!

**Eric**    Who was that lady I seen you with last night?

**Ernie**    You mean 'I saw'.

**Eric**    Sorry. Who was that eyesore I seen you with last night?

**Ernie**    Do you mind! When I first saw her at the Palais, she was easily the prettiest thing on the floor.

**Eric**    Yes, I can see her now, lying there.

**Ernie**    When I went to pick her up last night, she opened the door in her négligé!

**Eric**    That's a funny place to have a door.

**Ernie**   She's amazing! She's got everything a man could want.

**Eric**   Big muscles, a beard, a handlebar moustache . . .

**Ernie**   Her eyes are like two limpid pools!

**Eric**   . . . and her nose is like a diving board!

**Ernie**   Her ears are like petals.

**Eric**   Bicycle petals!

**Ernie**   Her cheeks are like peaches.

**Eric**   Football peaches!

**Ernie**   And her teeth are like stars.

**Eric**   They come out at night! I saw her in town last week wearing a miniskirt. Honestly, the last time I saw legs like that, there was a message tied to them! And those open-toed shoes she wears!

**Eric**   They're lovely!

**Ernie**   And very useful, too.

**Eric**   How d'you mean?

**Ernie**   I noticed her last night – with those open-toed shoes, she can pick up cigarette ends without bending down.

## Beside the Seaside, Beside the Sea!

**Ernie**  I bet you were glad to get here.

**Eric**  You're telling me! I stood outside the station and took a deep breath of that fresh seaside air.

**Ernie**  Marvellous!

**Eric**  One lung said to the other, 'That's the stuff I've been telling you about!'

**Ernie**  Great!

**Eric**  Then I went directly to the beach, stripped off and ran straight into the sea.

**Ernie**   Did It come up to your expectations?

**Eric**   Just past them actually – that's the trouble with being so short. Then, would you believe it, a crab bit my toe!

**Ernie**   Which one?

**Eric**   I don't know – all crabs look alike to me. Did you know I used to be a lifeguard?

**Ernie**   Really? When?

**Eric**   Last summer.

**Ernie**   What did you do?

> **Ernie** *My housemaid's knee has been giving me trouble.*
>
> **Eric** *Your housemaid's knee?*
>
> **Ernie** *Yes, the wife caught me sitting on it.*

**Eric** I saved women.

**Ernie** What for?

**Eric** The winter.

**Ernie** Didn't you help any men?

**Eric**   Yes, I gave them the occasional woman. One day I had to rescue a drunken mermaid.

**Ernie**   A drunken mermaid?

**Eric**   Yes, she'd had so much whisky on the rocks, she'd fallen into the sea.

**Ernie**   How drunk was she?

**Eric**   She was absolutely legless. I pulled her onto the beach and gave her artificial recreation.

**Ernie**   You mean artificial respiration. Recreation is when you have fun.

**Eric**   I'm no fool. She had a fabulous figure, too.

**Ernie**   Really?

**Eric**   Yes, thirty-six, twenty-three, eighty-five pence a pound.

## *Camping About!*

**Eric**   She's a lovely girl, though. I'd like to marry her, but her family objects.

**Ernie**   Her family?

**Eric**   Yes, her husband and four kids.

## Marry Making!

**Ernie** Ladies and gentlemen, 'The Wedding', a recitation:

**Eric** It seems like only yesterday that I got married. I wish it was tomorrow – I'd call the whole thing off.

**Ernie** To continue: 'On her finger a ring, on her face a smile,

**Eric** The radiant bride walks down the aisle . . .'

**Ernie** It was a love match pure and simple. I was pure and she was  simple.

**Eric** Do you mind! I'm trying to recite a poem . . .

**Ernie** The trouble was, I went into marriage with both eyes closed –

her father closed one and her brother closed the other.

**Eric**   Excuse me . . .

**Ernie**   I think they must have still been annoyed about our first wedding.

**Eric**   Your first wedding?

**Ernie**   Yes, it was a very quiet affair – I didn't turn up.

> **Eric**   *I've put the cat out.*
> **Ernie**   *What for?*
> **Eric**   *It was on fire.*

### *Honeymoonshine!*

**Ernie**  What did you go to Spain for?

**Eric**  Thirty-five pounds return. It was a honeymoon special.

**Ernie**  A honeymoon special? How long have you been married?

**Eric**  Three weeks. And they said it wouldn't last.

**Ernie**  But five weeks ago you didn't even have a girlfriend.

**Eric**  I know – our courtship was fast and furious.

**Ernie**  Really?

**Eric**  Yes – I was fast and she was furious.

**Ernie**  You took your wife into a topless
bar?

**Eric**  Yes. I mean – when you've seen two
you've seen them all. Anyway, it
turned out to be a bit of a
disappointment.

**Ernie**  How come?

**Eric**  Turned out to be a café with no roof
on. Still, we decided to eat there.
But just as they brought the food, it
started to rain.

**Ernie**  Oh no!

**Eric**  Oh yes – it took us an hour and a
half to finish the soup!

## The Dumb Waiter!

**Ernie**  Ah, good evening, I've been looking forward to patronising this restaurant.

**Eric**  Good evening, sir – and now we are looking forward to patronising you.

**Ernie**  Tell me – do you serve crabs?

**Eric**  We serve anyone, sir. Take a seat.

**Ernie**  Thank you, boy. I'm so hungry I could eat a horse.

**Eric**  You've certainly come to the right place, sir.

**Ernie**  Have you any wild duck?

**Eric**  No, sir – but we've got a tame one we could aggravate for you.

**Ernie**  Er, no thanks. Have you got pig's trotters?

**Eric**  No, sir – flat feet.

Eric: 'It never amazes me how so much talent can be supported on such short legs.'

## Losing His Patients!

**Ernie**   Doctor, I don't know what's wrong
with me. Do you think I'll ever get
better?

**Eric**   I don't know – let me feel your purse.

**Ernie**   But Doctor . . .

**Eric**   Sit down and tell me all about it . . .

**Ernie**   Doctor, I'm not a private patient.
I'm on the National Health.

**Eric**   . . . in less than two minutes.

**Ernie**   Well, for a start I've got this terrible
insomnia.

**Eric**   Well, I wouldn't lose any sleep over
it. Why don't you try eating
something before you go to bed?

**Ernie**  But Doctor – two months ago you told me never to eat anything before going to bed.

**Eric**  But that was two months ago – medical science has made enormous strides since then.

**Ernie**  I've been in bed all day with a hot water bottle and a thermometer in my mouth.

**Eric**  Well, there's certainly room enough for both.

**Ernie**  But what should I take for my cold?

**Eric**  Don't refuse any offer.

**Ernie**  But how can I stop it spreading from my head to my chest?

**Eric**    Tie a knot in your throat. And, incidentally, you need new glasses.

**Ernie**    How do you know?

**Eric**    I could tell as soon as you walked through that window.

**Ernie**    Well, aren't you going to examine me?

**Eric**    Certainly. Go over to the window and put your tongue out.

**Ernie**    Why?

**Eric**    'Cos I don't like the bloke who lives opposite.

**Ernie**    But do you think I'll live?

### The
### Handshake
*Hold out your right hand
as if to shake Ernie's hand.
As Ernie extends his right
hand, pull your right hand
up to push your spectacles
back on your nose and
turn away.*

**Eric**   We.. yes – but . . .

**Ernie**   But what?

**Eric**   . . . but I don't advise it.

## *Oh Doctor!*

**Ernie**  Ah, come in! You're coughing more easily this morning.

**Eric**  I should be – I've been practising all night.

**Ernie**  But aren't you taking the medicine I gave you?

**Eric**  No. I tasted it and I decided to keep coughing.

**Ernie**  But haven't you followed my advice for getting rid of a cold – to drink frozen orange juice after a hot bath?

**Eric**  Yes, but I haven't finished drinking the hot bath yet.

**Ernie**  Well, I've got a cold too, so cheer up, I've got the same complaint as you.

**Eric** True, but you are lucky in one respect.

**Ernie** What's that?

**Eric** You don't have the same doctor.

**Ernie** Well, I can't tell what's wrong with you. I think it's drink.

**Eric** Okay – I'll come back when you're sober.

**Ernie** Maybe you'd better give me a specimen.

**Eric**    OK.

**Ernie**    If you could just fill that bottle over there.

**Eric**    From here?

**Ernie**    Can you remember if your eyes have been checked before?

**Eric**    No, they've always been blue.

**Ernie**    Why do you wear those glasses?

**Eric**    I've got spots before my eyes.

**Ernie**    And do the glasses help?

**Eric**    Yes – the spots are much bigger now.

## Boxers Rule, KO?

**Eric** I was a pretty handy fighter in my youth. I could lick any man with one hand.

**Ernie** Really?

**Eric** Yes. Unfortunately, I could never find anyone with one hand who wanted a fight. All the same, I was a pretty colourful fighter.

**Ernie** How do you mean?

**Eric** I was black and blue all over. My best punch was my rabbit punch.

**Ernie** Yes?

**Eric** But they wouldn't let me fight rabbits.

# How to be like Eric & Ern:

### The Stripper Breakfast

*You'll need a copy of The Stripper theme, a kitchen, a kettle, two large oranges, two manual orange juicers (the kind that you rub the fruit into), four eggs, a frying pan, a pop-up toaster that can launch toast skywards, a large tub of margarine, two plates, a loaf of uncut bread, a bread knife, a butter knife, a string of sausages for use as a feather boa and the comic timing of two geniuses.*

## Court Napping!

**Ernie**  Order! Order in court!

**Eric**  Thank you, your honour. Mine's a pint of mild and bitter and a cheese sandwich.

**Ernie**  Name?

**Eric**  Duncan, sir.

**Ernie**  Duncan who?

**Eric**  Duncan Disorderly.

**Ernie**  Is this the first time you've been up before me?

**Eric**  I don't know – what time do you normally get up?

**Ernie**   Have you ever been cross-examined before?

**Eric**   Yes, your honour, I'm married.

**Ernie**   To how many wives?

**Eric**   Just the one, your honour. Honestly.

**Ernie**   In that case I'll drop that charge. That's bigamy.

**Eric**   It's very big of you, your honour.

**Ernie**   I'm going to teach you that crime doesn't pay.

**Eric**   I know it doesn't – but the hours are good.

*How to be like Eric:*

### The Spectacles

*Place your spectacles at an angle on the bridge of your nose so that the right lens is over the nose. Look at the camera and wiggle your eyebrows up and down.*

COMEDY CLASSICS

### Not Tonight, Josephine!

**Ernie**  Good evening, ladies and gentlemen. My name is Colonel Napoleon Davenport DSO, MC, OBE.

**Eric**  That's a funny way to spell Davenport.

**Ernie**  Are you maligning my decorations?

**Eric**  I never touched them!

**Ernie**  To continue: and I'm here tonight to tell you about my most famous ancestor, after whom I, Napoleon Davenport, am named.

**Eric**  No!

**Ernie**  Yes.

**Eric**  You're descended from . . .

**Eric**  *Red sky at night means that the shepherd's cottage is on fire.*

'This boy's a fool'

**Ernie**   That's right.

**Eric**   . . . Wilf Davenport, the legendary Stockport County centre-forward! This is fantastic! Let me shake your hand!

**Ernie**   You ignorant fool! I'm talking about Napoleon Bonaparte, Emperor of France. A brave fighter!

**Eric**   To continue: I have a painting of Napoleon at home. He's mounted on horseback and he's cutting a fine figure.

**Eric**   He's sitting on his sword!

## *Like No Business We Know!*

Ernie   Hello! Long time no see. How are you?

**Eric**   Fine, thanks.

Ernie   Got a job yet?

**Eric**   Got a terrific job.

Ernie   Great! What are you doing?

**Eric**   I work in the circus – mucking out the elephants.

Ernie   Mucking out the elephants? How many are there of them?

**Eric**   Twenty-five.

Ernie   Twenty-five elephants! How much do they pay you?

**Eric**    Seven pounds fifty a week.

**Ernie**    Seven pounds fifty a week for mucking out twenty-five elephants! That's terrible! If I were you, I'd chuck it all in and get an office job.

**Eric**    What, and give up show business?

**Ernie**    Is there any chance of advancement?

**Eric**    There might be – they've just fired the human cannonball. And they're looking for someone of the same calibre.

**Ernie**    Wait a minute – you were with the circus before. You were engaged to a lady contortionist. What happened?

**Eric**    She broke it off.

> **Ernie** *Something's just come up.*
> **Eric** *You're the lucky one.*

## Look at the Thighs of Her!

Ernie    But you told me the other day she had a million-dollar figure!

Eric    She has. Trouble is, it's all in loose change.

### She Dresses to Kill – and Cooks the Same Way!

**Ernie**   Why don't you wash your face – I can see what you had for breakfast this morning.

**Eric**   Really? What did I have?

**Ernie**   Bacon and eggs.

**Eric**   Wrong – that was yesterday morning. My wife was doing the cooking this morning so I settled for cornflakes. It's the only thing she can do.

**Ernie**   You must get sick of them.

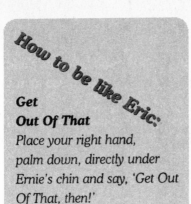

**How to be like Eric:**

**Get Out Of That**

*Place your right hand, palm down, directly under Ernie's chin and say, 'Get Out Of That, then!'*

**Eric**    I do. I've had so much cornflakes since I got married, I go soggy in the bath.

**Ernie**    Did you have to teach her how to prepare cornflakes?

**Eric**    I did. When we first got married she used to spoil them every time.

**Ernie**  How?

**Eric**  She used to boil them in the bag.

**Ernie**  Are things much different now?

**Eric**  Oh yes – I now know what it means to go home at night to a three-course slap-up supper.

**Ernie**  Really?

**Eric**  It means I've gone home to the wrong house, that's what it means.

## Party Lines!

**Eric**    Hello! Welcome to the party!

**Ernie**    I don't want to come to the party. I live downstairs and I've come up to complain about the row! I'm looking for the people who live here.

**Eric**    Well, you've certainly come to the right place.

**Ernie**    Didn't you hear me pounding on the ceiling?

**Eric**   Oh, that's OK – we were making a
lot of noise ourselves. We're
celebrating his granddad's one
hundred and third birthday.

**Ernie**   Really?

**Eric**   Yes. Pity his granddad can't be here
though.

**Ernie**   Why's that?

**Eric**   He died ten years ago. Still, it's not
bad for a Gay Nineties Party.

**Ernie**    A Gay Nineties Party? How d'you mean?

**Eric**    Well, all the men are gay and all the women are ninety. Do you drink?

**Ernie**    No.

**Eric**    Then hold this bottle while I tie my shoelaces.

COMEDY CLASSICS